Classy Clip Art

Illustrations by Dale Bargmann and Robert M. Moyer

Group *Books*
Loveland, Colorado

Classy Clip Art

Credits
Edited by Eugene C. Roehlkepartain
Cover and interior designed by Jill Christopher

Library of Congress Cataloging-in-Publication Data
Bargmann, Dale, 1947-
Classy clip art / illustrations by Dale Bargmann and Robert M. Moyer.
    p.
    Includes index.
    ISBN 1-55945-020-7
    1. Church bulletins. 2. Church newsletters—Publishing. 3. Copy art. I. Moyer,
    Robert M., 1924-   II. Title.
Bv653.3.B37   1991
254.3—dc20   91-14206
                                                                  CIP

Printed in the United States of America

Contents

Contents

Introduction

Imagine the scene when people receive their mail. They rummage through a whole stack of slick-looking magazines, "junk" mail with splashy art and headlines, and personal mail. And ... oh ... the youth group or church newsletter.

Will they pick it up? Can it really catch their attention in the midst of all the other material they receive?

With clip art from *Classy Clip Art* adding interest and a professional touch, the newsletter (or poster or flier or bulletin insert or handout) will get the attention it deserves. And you don't need art and design expertise to use it. Just follow these simple steps:

1. Write the information you want to convey. Keep it short and to the point. Include all important information for events and classes, including ...

● time;

● date; and

● place.

2. Select art for the item you want to illustrate. The index on page 121 will guide you to the specific topics illustrated in this book. The art is divided into the following categories:

● *Church Life*—Art for Sunday school, youth group, Bible study, worship, choir and other regular events in church life.

● *Special Events*—Art for special events, including talent shows, retreats, ski trips, sports, concerts and much more.

● *Hot Topics*—Art on youth-meeting topics, such as peer pressure, drugs, dating, love, family and more.

● *Service, Outreach and Missions*—Art for service ministries, including soup kitchens and visiting the elderly, people with disabilities and others.

● *Holidays, Seasons and Celebrations*—Art for everything from New Year's to Christmas to graduation.

● *Newsletters and Notes*—Dozens of tidbits to brighten up newsletters, including ready-to-use newsletter designs, greetings and more.

3. Type the information (or generate it on your computer) in the form you want, leaving room for the artwork. Think about creative ways to "wrap" the type around the art. Carefully read what you typed for clarity, accuracy and typographical errors.

4. Clip the right-size art. If you have a photocopier with enlargement and reduction capabilities, use it to make the art the exact size you need.

5. Glue the art into place. Using rubber cement will allow you to adjust the art without tearing it.

6. Duplicate and distribute the information. Then wait for people to notice the professional work!

Church Life

Church Life

BE A
CLOWN

BE A
CLOWN

BE A
CLOWN

**Make a
Noticeable Difference–
Join the Choir**

TAKE NOTE

TAKE NOTE

**Make a
Noticeable Difference–
Join the Choir**

**Make a
Noticeable Difference–
Join the Choir**

TAKE NOTE

VaCAtioN
BiBle SchooL

VaCAtioN
BiBle SchooL

VaCAtioN
BiBle SchooL

CELEBRATE!

IN TIMES OF NEED

IN TIMES OF NEED

WITH OUR PRAYERS

CELEBRATE!

IN TIMES OF NEED

CELEBRATE!

WITH OUR PRAYERS

WITH OUR PRAYERS

REACH OUT IN FELLOWSHIP

REACH OUT IN FELLOWSHIP

FATHER SON SPIRIT

ALLELUIA

FATHER SON SPIRIT

ALLELUIA

FATHER SON SPIRIT

ALLELUIA

REACH OUT IN FELLOWSHIP

Special Events

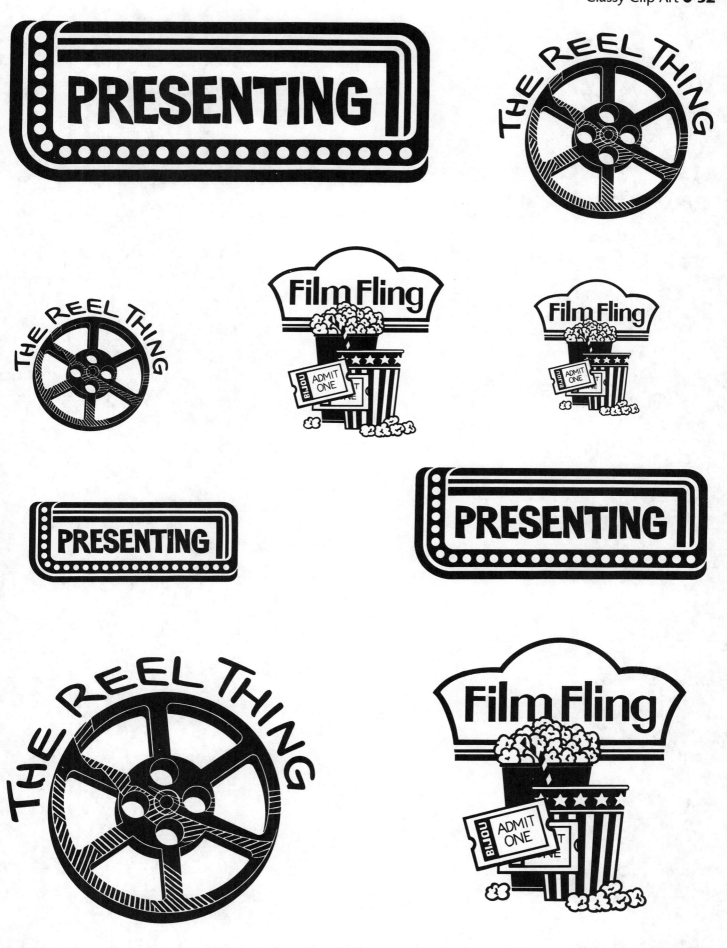

Take a Break

Take a Break

WE'LL WAIT UP FOR YOU

WE'LL WAIT UP FOR YOU

Take a Break

A GREAT WAY TO SPEND THE NIGHT

A GREAT WAY TO SPEND THE NIGHT

A GREAT WAY TO SPEND THE NIGHT

WE'LL WAIT UP FOR YOU

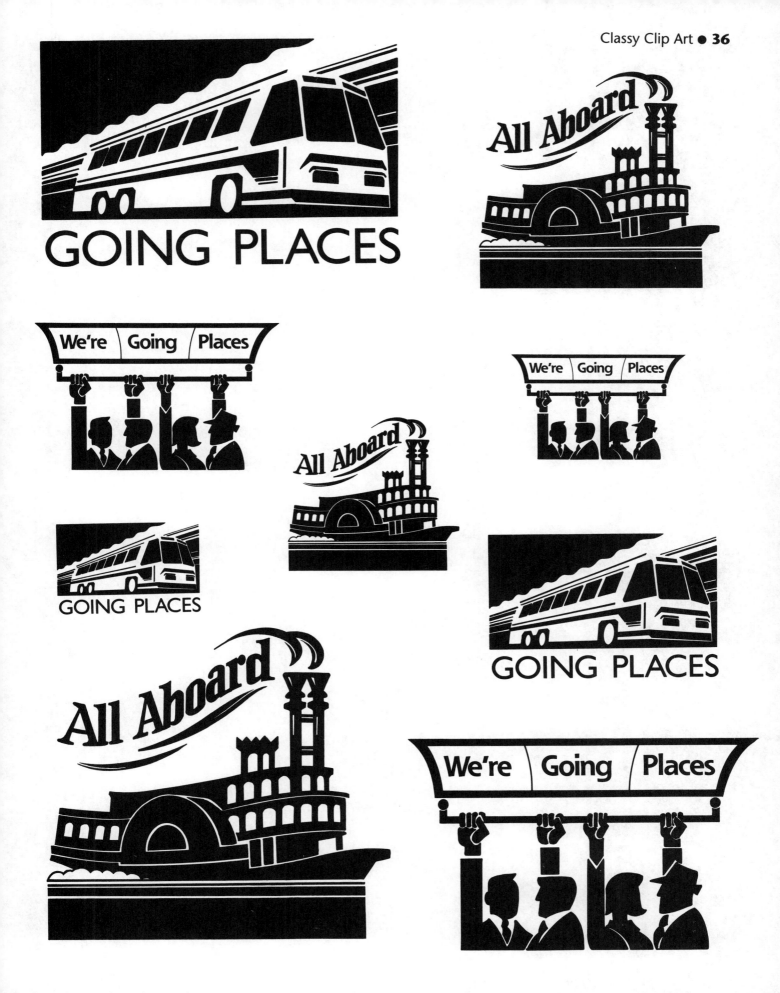

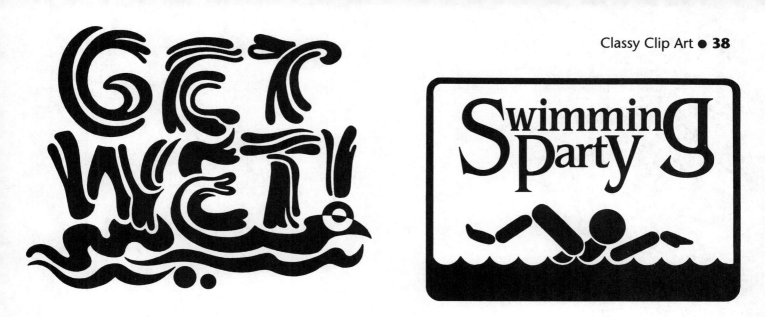

Raft-OAR Else

THE SKY'S THE LIMIT

THE SKY'S THE LIMIT

Raft-OAR Else

THE SKY'S THE LIMIT

Raft-OAR Else

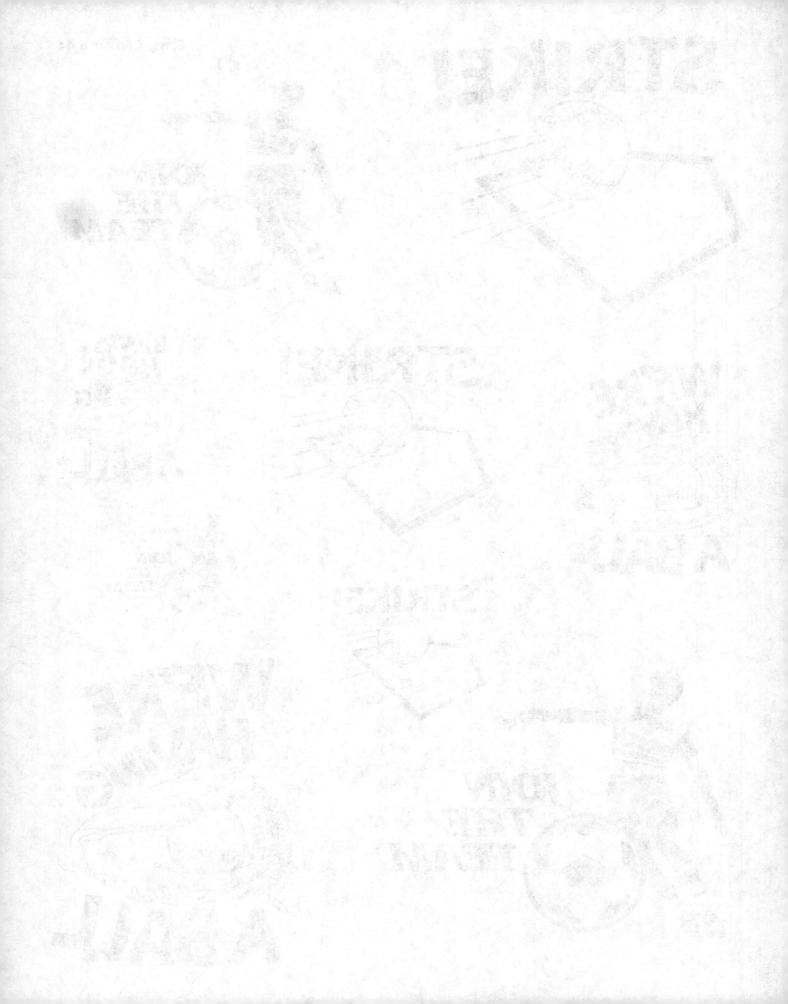

We're Having a Ball

We're Having a Ball

We're Having a Ball

We're Having a BALL!

We're Having a BALL!

We're Having a BALL!

Make Points With Us

Make Points With Us

Make Points With Us

Hot Topics

WHAT ARE FRIENDS FOR?

Do you fit in?

Lean on Me

WHAT ARE FRIENDS FOR?

WHAT ARE FRIENDS FOR?

Do you fit in?

Lean on Me

Lean on Me

Do you fit in?

CLASHING CLIQUES

CLASHING CLIQUES

CLASHING CLIQUES

All in the Family

ARE YOU
BOOKED
TONIGHT?

School
Daze

ARE YOU
BOOKED
TONIGHT?

School
Daze

ARE YOU
BOOKED
TONIGHT?

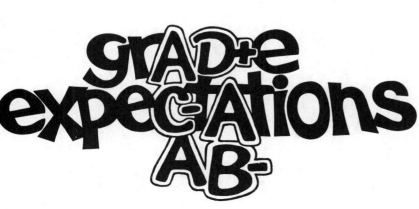

School
Daze

STRESSED OUT

STRESSED OUT

STRESSED OUT

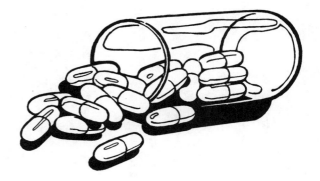

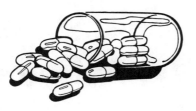

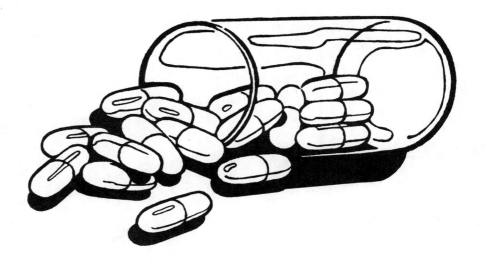

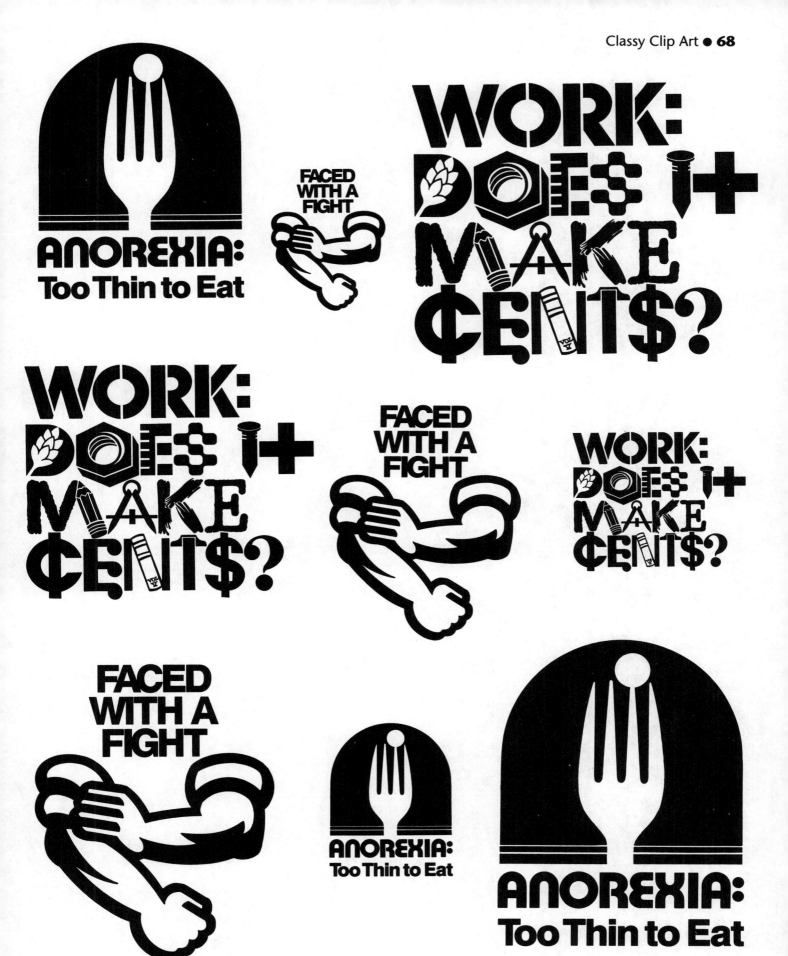

Service, Outreach and Missions

Need a friend?

Need a friend?

BUILDING IN FAITH

BUILDING IN FAITH

BUILDING IN FAITH

Care
For
The
Elderly

Care
For
The
Elderly

Care
For
The
Elderly

I WAS IN PRISON AND YOU CAME TO VISIT ME MATTHEW 25:36b

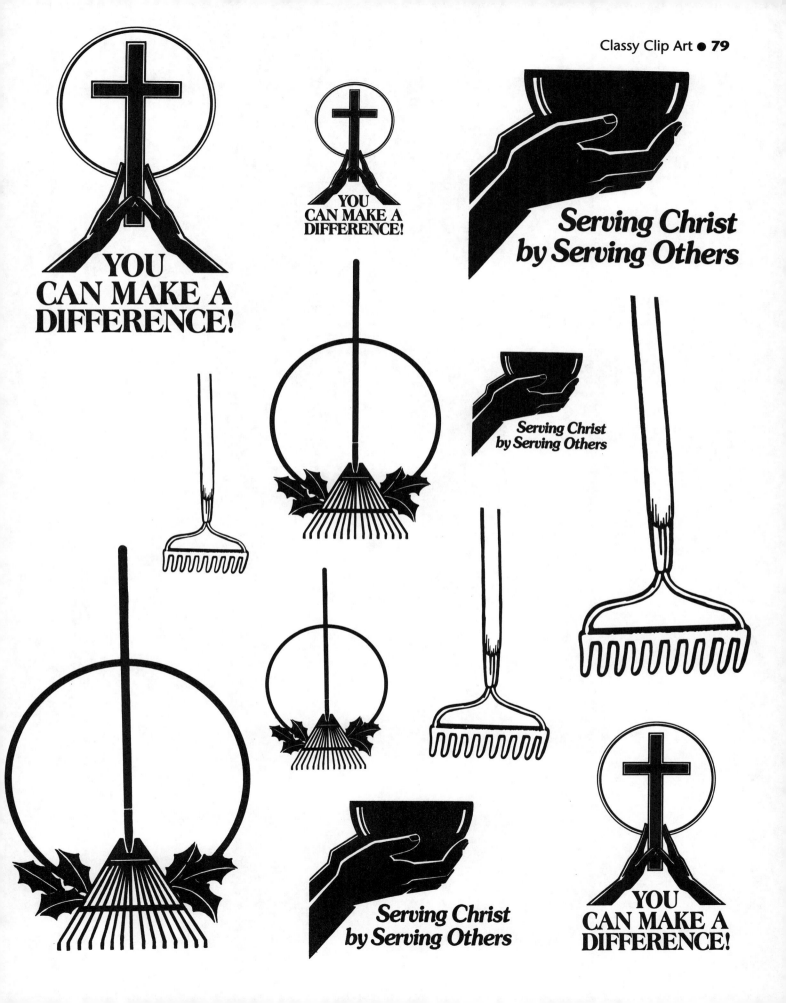

YOU CAN MAKE A DIFFERENCE!

YOU CAN MAKE A DIFFERENCE!

Serving Christ by Serving Others

Serving Christ by Serving Others

Serving Christ by Serving Others

YOU CAN MAKE A DIFFERENCE!

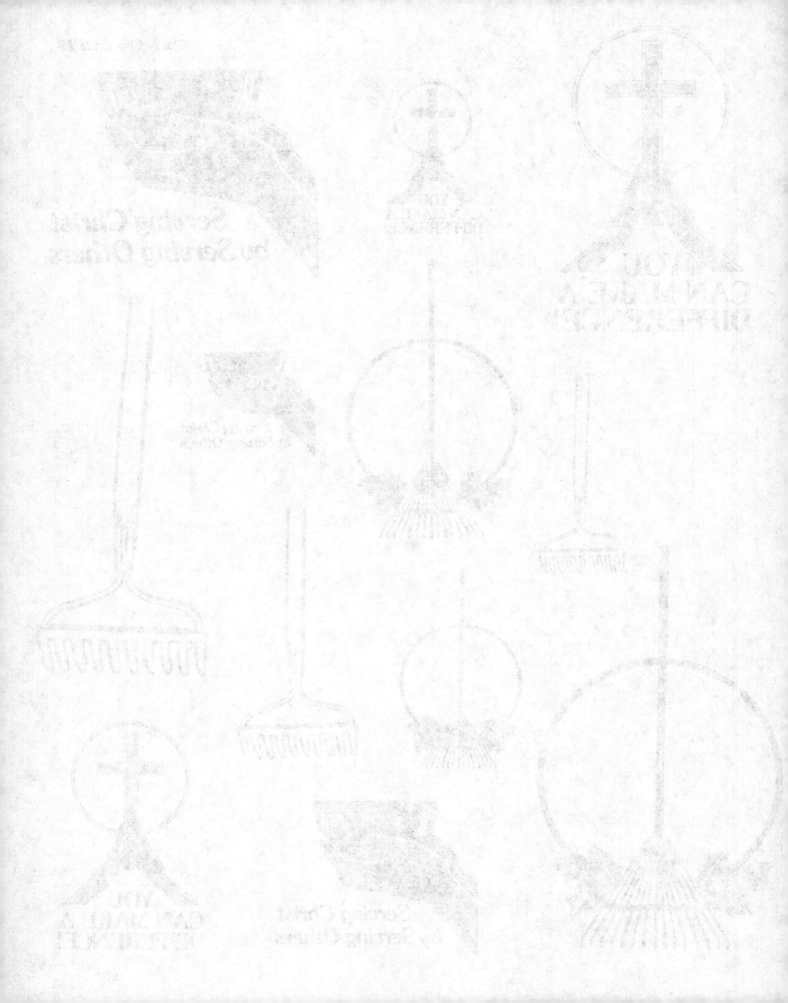

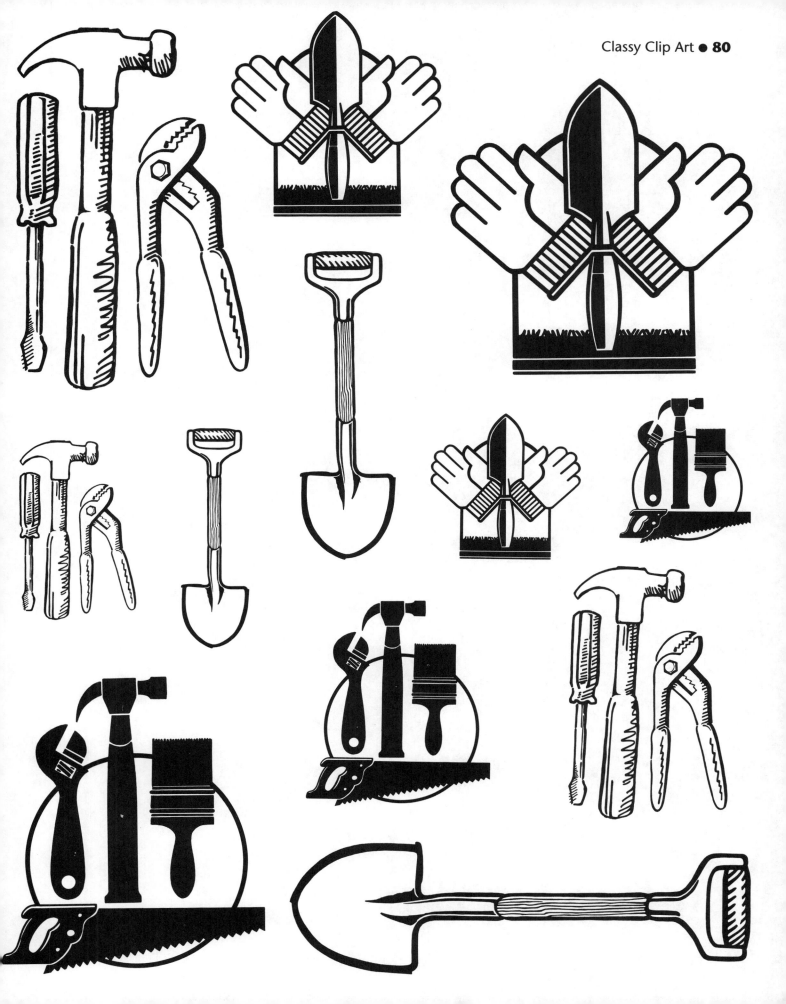

Holidays, Seasons and Celebrations

ST. PATRICK'S DAY

ST. PATRICK'S DAY

COME, HOLY SPIRIT

COME, HOLY SPIRIT

COME, HOLY SPIRIT

COME, HOLY SPIRIT

ST. PATRICK'S DAY

Maundy Thursday

GOOD FRIDAY

GOOD FRIDAY

He Died for Us

GOOD FRIDAY

Maundy Thursday

He Died for Us

He Died for Us

Maundy Thursday

Thanks, Dad

Love You, Dad

Independence DAY

Independence Day

Love You, Dad

Independence Day

Thanks, Dad

Thanks, Dad

Independence Day

Independence DAY

Independence DAY

Love You, Dad

HALLOWEEN: A TRICK OR A TREAT?

Fall Break

Fall Break

HALLOWEEN: A TRICK OR A TREAT?

HALLOWEEN: A TRICK OR A TREAT?

Take a Break

Take a Break

Take a Break

Fall Break

The gift of
Christmas

Merry Christmas

Merry Christmas

Merry Christmas

Newsletters and Notes

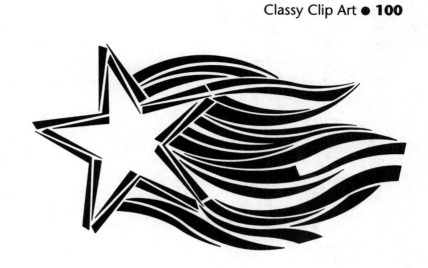

A STELLAR
PERFORMANCE!

A STELLAR
PERFORMANCE!

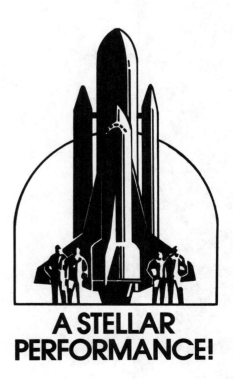

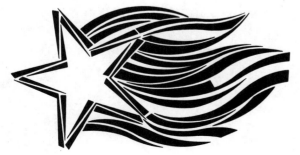

A STELLAR
PERFORMANCE!

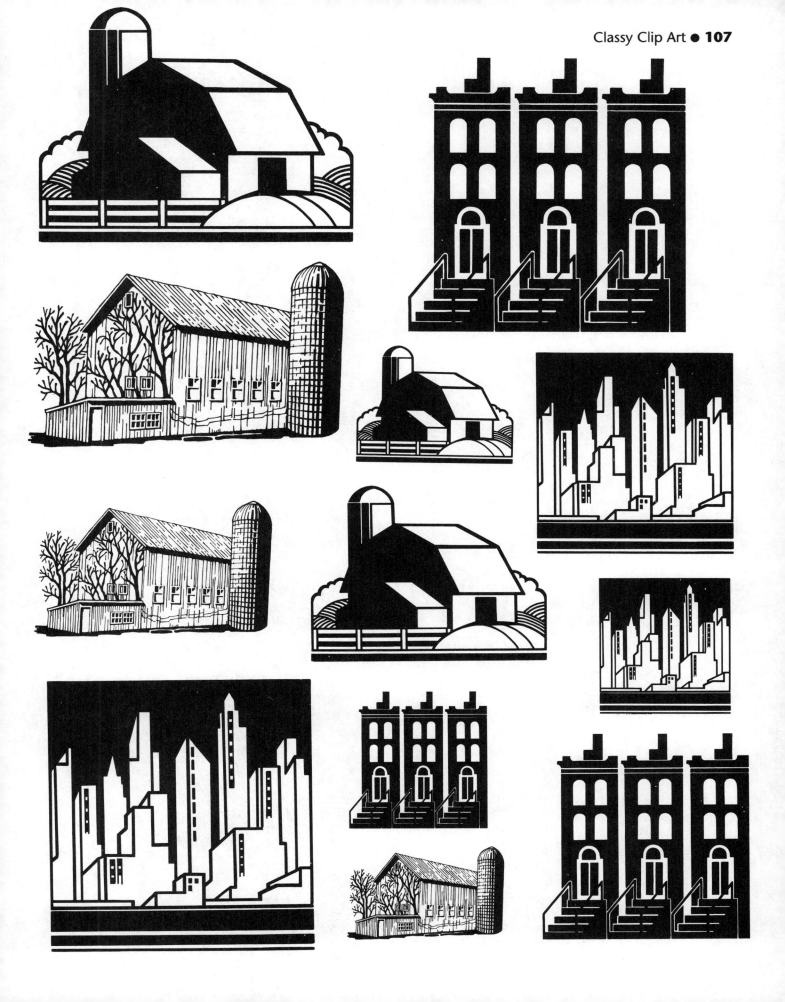

JANUARY
FEBRUARY
MARCH
APRIL
MAY
JUNE
JULY
AUGUST
SEPTEMBER
OCTOBER
NOVEMBER
DECEMBER

SUNDAY
MONDAY
TUESDAY
WEDNESDAY
THURSDAY
FRIDAY
SATURDAY

SUNDAY
MONDAY
TUESDAY
WEDNESDAY
THURSDAY
FRIDAY
SATURDAY

SUNDAY   MONDAY
TUESDAY   WEDNESDAY
THURSDAY   FRIDAY
SATURDAY

JANUARY	JULY
FEBRUARY	AUGUST
MARCH	SEPTEMBER
APRIL	OCTOBER
MAY	NOVEMBER
JUNE	DECEMBER

SUNDAY
MONDAY
TUESDAY
WEDNESDAY
THURSDAY
FRIDAY
SATURDAY

JANUARY
FEBRUARY
MARCH
APRIL
MAY
JUNE
JULY
AUGUST
SEPTEMBER
OCTOBER
NOVEMBER
DECEMBER

JANUARY
FEBRUARY
MARCH
APRIL
MAY
JUNE
JULY
AUGUST
SEPTEMBER
OCTOBER
NOVEMBER
DECEMBER

JANUARY
FEBRUARY
MARCH
APRIL
MAY
JUNE

JULY
AUGUST
SEPTEMBER
OCTOBER
NOVEMBER
DECEMBER

JANUARY
FEBRUARY
MARCH
APRIL
MAY
JUNE

JULY
AUGUST
SEPTEMBER
OCTOBER
NOVEMBER
DECEMBER

Index

Even More Great Clip Art from *Group*

SEASONAL CLIP-ART

Your church's publicity will stand out season after season with these ready-to-go designs. You'll make...
- professional-looking posters that attract crowds to your special programs,
- nifty newsletters that share your church's seasonal news,
- fabulous fliers to remind members of upcoming events,
- bright bulletins to showcase your worship services,

...and more! Plus, illustrations are varied in style and form to fit whatever design you're trying to match.

Seasonal Clip-Art is quick and easy to use. Find your season in the table of contents, pick the design and size you need, and photocopy for instant use! The creative results will attract attention and help build your ministry.

ISBN 1-55945-178-5

CHILDREN'S MINISTRY CLIP ART

Mary Lynn Ulrich

Add pizazz and style to your ministry with creative clip art. Use these lively illustrations in newsletters, fliers, letters, and on bulletin boards—anywhere you need to grab kids'—and parents'—attention.

With this creative art, you can...
- design fabulous fliers and handouts for meetings on dozens of topics,
- announce upcoming events with zany, attention-getting calendars, and
- promote specific children's ministry programs.

This giant collection of clip art will add a professional touch to your children's ministry. It's as easy as 1-2-3.

    1—Choose your art   2—Cut it out   3—Paste it down

and your publicity is ready to photocopy!

ISBN 1-55945-018-5

YOUTH MINISTRY CLIP ART

You'll get hundreds of pieces of ready-to-use artwork—in all kinds of sizes. Headlines. Cartoons. Borders. Everything you need to jazz up your printed pieces. Discover creative new ways to build enthusiasm for...
- special activities—trips, retreats, and holidays;
- meetings—dozens of topics including Bible studies, discipleship, peer pressure, and more; and
- increasing attendance—calendars and reminders.

Using clip art is as easy as 1-2-3! First, choose your art. Second, cut it out. Third, paste it on the page. Then, head to the nearest photocopier and turn out professional-looking and attention-grabbing newsletters, handouts, posters, fliers, and more! Plus, you'll find easy-to-follow directions, a fast index, and lots of suggestions to make your announcements shout!

ISBN 0-931529-26-3

Order today from your local Christian bookstore, or write: Group Publishing, Box 485, Loveland, CO 80539. For mail orders, please add postage/handling of $4 for orders up to $15, $5 for orders of $15.01+. Colorado residents add 3% sales tax.

A Practical, Easy-to-Teach Curriculum for Adults

Apply-It-To-Life™ Adult Bible Series offers adult groups...

*ACTIVE LEARNING!
Apply-It-To-Life™ Adult Bible Series teaches as Jesus taught—with *active learning*. Participants get involved in experiences and learn to share with others in the group—rather than listening to a lecture.

*REAL LIFE ISSUES!
Lessons help connect scriptural truths to real life. Then, through group interaction, discovery, and discussion, adults will...
- learn from each other's experiences how to grow closer to God,
- dig into the Scriptures and come away with a personal application of the passages,
- explore how God works through relationships, and
- learn what it means to be a Christian in today's world.

*NO STUDENT BOOKS—EASY FOR TEACHERS!
Each **Apply-It-To-Life™** topic is covered in four lessons. Change the topic after four weeks, or mix and match other titles in the series to provide your class with a variety of challenging and interesting topics. Everything you need for any-size class is included to make your job a breeze: complete leaders guide, handout masters you can photocopy, publicity helps, and bonus ideas. Plus, your teaching commitment is only four weeks!

*LOW COST!
Because there are no student books to buy, the cost per adult is minimal—and the books can be used over and over, year after year! Offer classes the adults in your church will enjoy—and save money at the same time!

Put your adult education in a new direction—order **Apply-It-To-Life™ Adult Bible Series** today!

The Church: What Am I Doing Here?	ISBN 1-55945-294-3
Communication: Enhancing Your Relationships	ISBN 1-55945-297-8
Evangelism for Every Day	ISBN 1-55945-298-6
Faith in the Workplace	ISBN 1-55945-299-4
Marriage: Choosing a Lifetime Partner	ISBN 1-55945-296-X
Revelation: Unlocking Its Secrets	ISBN 1-55945-295-1

Order today from your local Christian bookstore, or write: Group Publishing, Box 485, Loveland, CO 80539. For mail orders, please add postage/handling of $4 for orders up to $15, $5 for orders of $15.01+. Colorado residents add 3% sales tax.